Katherine Grace
Unlocks the Keys

Written by
JoAnn Nocera

Illustrated by
Cheryl Mendenhall

Note to Parents:

This children's book is a perfect companion to *Give Me Back My Crayons*. In the adult book, there are "Creative Cues" at the end of each chapter to help guide you and your child through a creative experience. You can share all the ways to unlock your creativity together using this children's book as your guide to explaining the 10 Keys. Additionally, we hope this book brings out valuable conversations and diminishes feelings of inadequacy or self-doubt.

Book Club Discussions:

What does Katherine Grace love to do?

Why doesn't Katherine Grace like her potholder at first?

What should Katherine Grace do to help her friends disconnect from their devices?

If you and Katherine Grace were friends what would you do together?

There are 10 hidden keys to creativity. Look for the key 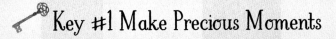 in each illustration and discuss what it means:

🔑 Key #1 Make Precious Moments

🔑 Key #2 Be Present, Not Perfect

🔑 Key #3 Set Up Your Space

🔑 Key #4 Learning is Messy

🔑 Key #5 Put the Device Away

🔑 Key #6 No Instructions Necessary

🔑 Key #7 One Size Does Not Fit All

🔑 Key #8 It's About the Process, Not the Product

🔑 Key #9 Always Look Up

🔑 Key #10 Celebrate Your Unique Self

Published by Inspired Girl Books
www.inspiredgirlbooks.com

Inspired Girl Books is honored to bring forth books with heart and stories that matter.
We are proud to offer this book to our readers; the story, the experiences, and the words are the author's alone.

ISBN: 978-1-7373163-1-2 (paperback)
978-1-7373163-2-9 (hardcover)

Typesetting by Roseanna White Designs

Library of Congress Control Number: 2021942245

To creative children everywhere ~
you are a jewel to this world ~ shine ever so brightly!

Do you ever feel like some days can last forever?
Like it's the best day of your life and you didn't even go anywhere fancy?
Grandma says some days are like that and some days are not.
But everyday we can make precious moments.

Mom says I need to sit properly on the couch.

Sometimes I'm Grandma's helper, and sometimes I'm a "maker."
To be a "maker" you have to have lots of courage
even if it doesn't turn out the way you wanted.

"How come mine doesn't look like yours?" I say.

But Grandma says, "When you're a maker, Katherine,
it's about being present, not perfect."
We spend hours talking and laughing and all of a sudden
those bad thoughts go away.

I can be
myself!

And that's okay!

Today Mom and I set up a space
for me upstairs. My crayons, paints,
buttons, brushes, markers, and yarn
will finally have a home of their own.

But then I thought,
"What if I want to be creative
in the kitchen or the living room
or with my friends?"

Mom says,
"Creativity has a home
wherever you go!"

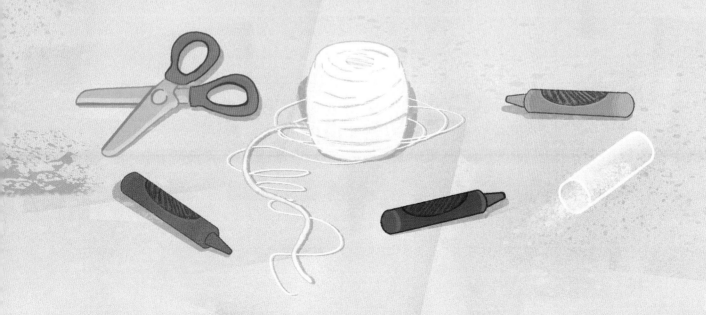

Chirp! Chirp!

The little birdie sings.
My friends don't hear a thing!
They just keep on tapping, scrolling, and yelling at their screens!
What's fun about that?
This isn't creative! I wish they would put their devices away!

"Let's go outside and play!"
Should I shout and scream?

21

My friends Justin, Tori, and I love to explore to find treasures.
No instructions necessary!

Creativity is like that, you know...
If you don't give up on it...it just happens.
Just like that!

Sometimes my friends and I can't decide what to do next.
We sit in the garden and then it comes to us.
One Size Does Not Fit All!
We can all do different things and still be together.

Bubbles are like big and small bursts of joy!
Sometimes they pop so fast,
I don't get a chance to see their beautiful colors.
So I slow down just enough to enjoy them a little bit.
Mom tells me that sometimes the most beautiful things
are hidden amongst the smallest moments.
She says it's about the process not the product—
whatever that means?!?!

Sometimes we take car rides and gaze at the beautiful seascape.

It's just a short ride to the campgrounds,
but if we look closely we can make it last forever.

Not every day can be the best day ever.
Sometimes I feel scared and can't figure things out,
but then I look up. I remember the story my grandma told me...

Long ago, in a country far away, there lived a wise old man. Every night he would gather up all his precious jewels and place them in an old chest. Each jewel was made up of his memories for the day.

Each day when he would begin his journey, he would take one grain of salt and place it in his pocket. For every moment, a new jewel would appear. Some were fancy and had lots of shine and glitter, and some jewels were dark and cloudy. But he continued to place them in the chest at the end of the day.

One afternoon, a witch appeared and stole his chest of jewels. Big or small, brilliant or cloudy, the moments belonged to the old man.

The witch became very angry when she realized the jewels had no value to her. So she cast them into the sky to rid them forever, but they emerged as stars!

Celebrations are the BEST!
Everything STOPS and we make time to enjoy
all the things we made.

"Gifts," Grandma says, "that were meant to make
the world a better place."

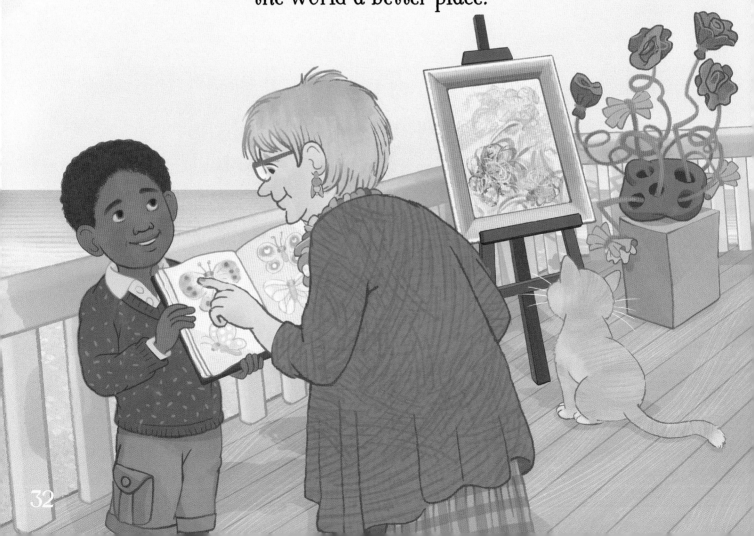

33

In and Around New Jersey:

Sunset Park, Harvey Cedars, NJ
www.harveycedars.org

Colorful Houses:
Taylor Ave, Beach Haven, NJ

Driftwood Sculptures

References/Resources:

Directions for QR Codes:

1. Open your phone camera
2. Place your camera over the QR Code and a link will appear
3. Tap the link on your phone

How to Make a Hand Knit blanket

Weaving Using a Mini Loom

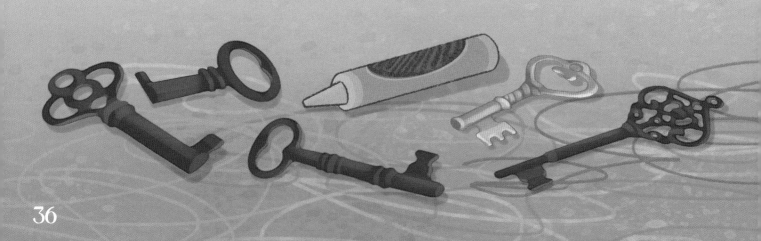

Fisherman's Cove Conservation Area,
Manasquan, NJ

Sea Turtles in NJ